A Journey

Two Souls into One

Tony Henninger

inner child press, ltd.

General Information

A Journey Of Love

Two Souls into One

Tony Henninger

1st Edition : 2013

This Publishing is protected under Copyright Law as a "Collection". All rights for all submissions are retained by the Individual Author and or Artist. No part of this Publishing may be Reproduced, Transferred in any manner without the prior **WRITTEN CONSENT** of the "Material Owner" or its Representative Inner Child Press. Any such violation infringes upon the Creative and Intellectual Property of the Owner pursuant to International and Federal Copyright Law. Any queries pertaining to this "Collection" should be addressed to Publisher of Record.

Publisher Information
1st Edition : Inner Child Press
intouch@innerchildpress.com
www.innerchildpress.com

This Collection is protected under U.S. and International Copyright Laws

Copyright © 2013 : Tony Henninger
LOC : 1-876044677

ISBN-13 : 978-0615754758
ISBN-10 : 0615754759

$ 9.00

Acknowledgments

I would like to give my deepest thanks to Mr. William S. Peters Sr. for his staunch support, his inspiration, and his beautiful spirit. He is such a blessing to us all.

I would, also, give credit to Janet Caldwell and Jill Delbridge for their beautiful hearts and love of writing.

Last, I would like to give my appreciation to all the wonderful poets in the Artist Lounge whose poetry inspired me to "get on with it", as Bill would say.

Without these wonderful people in my life this book might never have been put together.

Thank you all from the bottom of my heart.

BLESSINGS!!!

Tony

Deanne & Tony

Dedication

For my wife, Deanne,

I love you, forever!

Tony

Table of Contents

Acknowledgments — iv
About The Author — viii

Falling

Walking	2
A Glimpse Of Hope	3
Our Own World	4
Endlessly	5
Only Me	6
I Would Love You …	7
What I Want	8
Tonight	10
Only You	11
Missing You	12
Just A Note	14
Waiting To Love You	15
All I Want	17
Lets…	19

In Love

Until I Met You	22

Table of Contents... *continued*

The One Love	23
If Not For You	25
A Love Like This	26
In The Misty Morning	28
All The Way	30
Never Say Goodbye	31
You Make It All O.K.	32
I Love You	33

With You

Safe Within Our Love	36
More Than My Dreams	37
Sea Of Dreams	38
A Moment In Heaven	40
Nothing	42
You	43
You II	44
Every Time	45
Realization	46
Our Love - The Brightest Star	47
Reflection	48
Soul Mates	49

About the Author

Tony was born in Frankfurt, Germany. He now resides in Texas with his wife and son, a cat, and two dogs.

Tony Henninger

A Journey Of Love

Two Souls into One

Tony Henninger

inner child press, ltd.

Falling

a Journey of Love

Walking

In my darkest hour
Yours is the only light I see.
Though you are far away,
It keeps me alive.

I don't know if
It could ever be that
I might find you
Here beside me,

But, I am walking
A path of dreams
And nightmares
I know is leading me to you.

Perhaps,
Someday,
Someway,
We can live
In our light
Of love

Forever.

Tony Henninger

A Glimpse of Hope

Underneath a rainbow,
I saw you standing there,
With sparkling eyes and
Flowing satin hair.

Your eyes saw straight through
To my soul and eased my pain
Of loneliness as I reached for you.
But my reaching was in vain.

For here I am,
Alone once again,
To face my world
Of clouds and rain.

But, I have hope, that
Maybe soon, someday,
You will come in a dream again
And take all my sorrows away.

Our Own World

Close your eyes
And disappear with me
Into a world
Only we can see.

Listen to my voice
And follow it where
My love is waiting
For you there.

Feel my breath
Caress your soft skin.
Feel the fire
Burning within.

Turn around
And you will see
What you thought
Was only fantasy.

We start with
A grain of sand
Using our imagination
To build

Our own world.

Tony Henninger

Endlessly

Sometime I wonder what it's all about.
The silver lining of a cloud.
The fourth leaf of a clover.
Too soon, I know, it is over.

Maybe we have known each other,
In many times and many places,
Always meeting each other again;
Only wearing different faces.

Our souls always searching,
Finding ourselves anew.
Falling in love again and again.
Making One out of Two.

If you look into my eyes,
In the reflection you will see,
A flame that burns for you
Forever and ever;

Endlessly.

a Journey of Love

Only Me

See only me
Whenever life blinds you.
Call to only me
Whenever you feel lost.
Run to only me
Whenever you feel distant.
Cling to only me
Whenever you are frightened.
Hold on to only me
Whenever you need strength.
Talk to only me
Whenever you need someone to listen.
Touch only me
Whenever you are lonely.
Sleep with only me
Whenever you want to dream.
Love only me
Whenever your heart is in need.
Imagine only me
Whenever you want a fantasy.
Know only my soul
Whenever you look into the sun.
Find only me
Whenever you seek

True love.

Tony Henninger

I Would Love You

I would love you

On a bed of rose-thorns

That I might relish

The pain with the ecstasy.

I would love you

On the surface of the sun

That I might feel your love

burn hotter than any star.

I would love you

On the tallest peak

That I might know no love

Is higher than your love.

I would love you

Until forever

That I might taste

Heaven.

What I Want

What I want?
A question never asked until now.
Should I hide from this?
Behind this long-standing wall?

So many years lost
In some forgotten reverie.
Believing, to stay hidden, was
The only way to be free.

Better not tell anyone about me.
Never show anyone how I feel.
Better to keep things to myself.
The only way to feel real.

And now, you show me love.
Now you've opened the door.
You wish to give me all I want
As my wall crumbles to the floor.

Tony Henninger

I want you always beside me.
I want to breathe in your scent.
I want to always love you
Until my mind and body are spent.

I want to shout out "I Love You!"
No matter who might hear me.
I want to show you my soul.
All the beauty there is to see.

I want to be who I am.
I want you to be who you are.
I want to sparkle in your eyes.
I want to give you the stars.

I want us to live forever,
Loving each other more each day.
I want to always make you smile
Whether I am near or far away.

I want us to be honest.
I want us to be true.
But, most of all, I want
To be everything for you.

a Journey of Love

Tonight

If I want someone tonight,
I know I only want you.

If I need someone tonight,
I know I only need you.

If I fall tonight,
I want to fall into you.

If I can hold you tonight,
I open my arms to you.

If I give my heart tonight,
I give my heart to you.

If I could have one wish tonight,
I wish to make love to you.

If I sleep tonight,
I want to sleep with you.

If I have dream tonight,
I know I will dream of you.

If the end comes tonight,
I want to spend it with you.

If I say only one thing tonight,
I know it must be
"I Love You!"

Tony Henninger

Only You

When I dream,
I dream of only you.
When I see beauty,
I see only you.
When I want love,
I want only you.
When I need love,
I need only you.
When I get scared,
I hold on to only you.
When I need to cry,
I cry for only you.
When I laugh,
I laugh with only you.
When I am happy,
I am happy because of only you.
When my soul yearns,
It yearns for only you.
When my heart bleeds,
It bleeds for only you.
When I die,
I will wait for only you.

My heart belongs to only you.

For me,
There is,
Only
You.

Missing You

Missing you is the hardest thing for me to do.
Everyday I watch as you slowly drive away.
I know it is hard for you too.
I can see it in your eyes.
The love you feel shines through
The tears that begin to rise.
We are like two shadows
Chasing rainbows
Behind closed doors.
And in my dreams
It's just not the same.
I miss your touch.
To hear you say my name.
To feel the heat of
Your need and mine.
Your skin so soft.
Your lips so sweet,
Like fine wine.
I can't get enough of you,
The one I love.
Holding you in my arms so tight,
I know it's right.
Feeling our hearts beat as one,

Tony Henninger

The heat in our blood flowing faster.
Anticipating.
Release.
I can see, me,
In your arms in ecstasy.
Day by day, I find my way
To you and your heart.
Come and grow old with me.
The best is yet to be.
I'm ready to start with you.
I give you all I have to give.
My life, my love, my soul.
You're the reason I was meant to live.
You've captured my most precious heart
In your loves embrace.
Never let it go.
Always keep it safe.
Love comes to those who believe
And I believe in ours completely.
I am not afraid to see
What lies beyond reality.
Neverending, everlasting,
As it was meant to be.
I love you,
Eternally.

Just A Note

I'm not looking forward to

The night I'll spend

Without you near me,

But, I'll see you in my dreams.

What you give me I keep

For these moments alone.

I know the sky is fading

And time is flying by.

I can never tell you

All I need to,

But, I'm giving it a try

Through my writings.

Tony Henninger

Waiting To Love You

In the quiet solitude of my heart
Lies my soul as it dreams of you.
Biding its time in darkness until
Your love comes shining through.

Once, in a dream, I saw you standing there
Looking into my aching heart.
Your lips on mine making me dream
Of a time we won't be apart.

When I can taste your sweet love
And kiss your every tender spot.
Make love as if time did not exist
And be the ember that keeps you hot.

Touching all of your five horizons
As we embrace in ecstasy.
Surrounded by an aura of love
Fulfilling our every need.

a Journey of Love

When you look at me I always see
What I have been searching for.
When I feel lost you find me and
I am not lost anymore.

In all this chaotic reality
You are my deepest fantasy.
My hopes, my sweetest dream,
All I could ever need.

Thank you for letting me see
The beauty and love that is you.
The love that is in me
Has been waiting for you.

I want to give you everything you need.
I want to love you in every way and more.
I'll be waiting here, inside my heart,
Wanting only to love you

Forevermore.

Tony Henninger

All I Want

I arrived home from my morning walk
Thinking of you the entire time.
Of falling in love with you and
Wanting you to be mine.

I was so tired, so tired of everything.
Like the cold dead of a winter's snow
Covering my heart with a sleepy surrender
Leaving only a small dull glow.

The fears, the loneliness, and the tears,
Were hidden by wearing my disguise.
No one could ever see through
The fake smile of my eyes.

For so long have I waited and cried out
In the dark for someone to
hear my lamentations of sorrow.
For a life that seemed to be done.

Not knowing what my future holds,
So exciting, yet frightening too.
Finally getting up the nerve to say
How I felt and that I love you.

It felt natural to say those words
As you looked at me with questioning eyes.
Thinking, could he be the one for me?
Has he answered my own cries?

I've loved you for a long time.
In my soul I know it's true.
I am the one you've been searching for
And I am not afraid of loving you.

a Journey of Love

I've made love to you in my dreams.
We've circled the sun in our embrace.
We've flown on wings of love to heaven
And were blessed by Gods grace.

In every lifetime your true love exists.
When you discover each other, it is bliss.
All the crying, all the pain falls away,
Like a snowflake melts with a kiss.

You melted my pain and anguish away.
No more escaping into dreams of sin.
No more teardrops on red roses
Since you let my love in.

I'm so blessed to have found you,
Words fail me to really explain,
How my soul shines with delight
To have love's feeling again.

Nothing can stop our love from growing
Into the deep unending kind
That poets have often spoken of,
But is so hard to find.

If the world should end tomorrow
I would spend the end with you.
Looking forward to our own heaven
Especially made for me and you.

Such lofty thoughts I have.
Such a grand design I see.
Love has finally found us.
Forever our love will be.

Tony Henninger

Lets…

Speak to me of love as you

Fall into my embrace.

Swim into the depth of my ocean

And let your heart race.

Let me show you my dreams.

Let me fulfill all of your fantasies today.

I will whisper sweet words of desire

And make your body sway.

Ask nothing, ask everything,

Let your heart soar.

Think of nothing but love.

Love, Love, Love, Forevermore.

a Journey of Love

In Love

a Journey of Love

Until I Met You

Before I met you,
I thought I was happy.
And I was.
But, I had never known
Such rich contentment,
Deep satisfaction.
And total fulfillment,
You brought to me when
You came into my life.

Before I met you,
I felt many things.
Good things.
But, I had never experienced
The indescribable and intense
Feelings I have for you.

Before I met you,
I thought I knew myself.
And I did.
But, you looked deep inside of me
And found fresh new things.

Before I met you,
I thought I knew about love.
But, I didn't.

Until I met you.

Tony Henninger

The One Love

Did I tell you that you are beautiful?
I want to each and every day.
In the darkest recesses of my soul
Your light melts all the shadows away.

When I look into your eyes, I see,
The woman I have been dreaming of.
Oh, how you please and comfort me
When you give me of your love.

When I taste your sweet kisses,
Your arms open wide,
There is a fever that burns in me.
It burns so deep inside.

With you, I feel, I am living
A thousand lives in one.
When I touch you my hands tremble,
My heart begins to run.

Your lovely hair, oh, how it tingles
Whenever it touches my skin.
I am so in love with you,
More than I have ever been.

I am holding heaven in my arms,
When I am holding you.
As high as the sky, as deep as the sea,
So much love I feel for you.

a Journey of Love

I want to always stand by your side
And kiss your tears and pain away.
I want to hold you in my arms
And make you believe in me every day.

You know I love you and
So much more I want to give.
To be in your light and heart
Is all I need to live.

You are the one heart I am following.

The one wish that keeps me trying.

The one dream that keeps me wondering.

The One Love

that keeps me believing.

Tony Henninger

If Not For You

If not for you,
I would not know
What true love really meant.
I would never feel this inner peace.
I could not be content.

If not for you,
I would never have
The pleasure of romance.
I would miss the bliss, the craziness,
Of love's sweet silly dance.

I have to feel your tender touch.

I have to hear your voice.

No other could ever take your place.

For me, there is no other choice.

If not for you,
I would be adrift.
I don't know what I would do.
Always searching for my other half.

Incomplete.

If not for you.

A Love Like This

Once I thought I would never find you.
Once I thought we could never be.
Once I thought the end was coming.
Once I thought it was the end of me.

Some days the rain felt good.
Some days it made me feel sad.
I think of all the time I've wasted.
The things I could have had.

I have lived my life deep in shadow
Wanting for just one dream to come true.
Then, I saw you and my illusions scattered
Like dark clouds as my sky turned blue.

"Come with me for a moment", you said.
"Let me show what is inside of me.
Let the sky fall far behind us.
There is so much I want you to see."

Now, all those shadows have left me.
My eyes are open wide.
As the world keeps on spinning below us,
I realize, all I need is you by my side.

In your eyes I see the starlight
Of a thousand suns burning bright.
That is how your love feels to me
In my heart every day and every night.

Tony Henninger

I feel so lucky. I feel so grateful.
I wish to thank the powers that be
For showing me that dreams do come true.
For sending an angel like you to me.

Like the flowers I give to you,
The colors of my soul like a rainbow.
There they will last for an eternity.
I love you so much, you know.

To find a love like this in my lifetime
Is all I've been asking for.
Now that we are together as one
My heart will love you forevermore.

In The Misty Morning

In the misty morning,
While waiting for you,
I watch the dawning sky
As it begins to turn blue.

In the briskness of the day,
Drifting on a daydream away,
I wonder what I would do
If there was no me and you.

My heart would always be missing
The love that makes it whole.
I would sit in quiet despair
As ice grew around my soul.

I would live my life, day after day,
Not letting anyone grab a hold.
Your love takes all that away.
The loneliness, the pain, and the cold.

You are all I will ever need.
You are my only source of heat.
When I feel cold and lonely
You are my one and only.

Tony Henninger

Your beauty shines so bright,
Like all the stars at night.
And I love to hear you say
You love me anyway.

When all is said and done
I know we will be as one.
Two hearts melting together.
Our love shining forever.

And, in this misty morning,
Though constrained by time,
We stand hand in hand together.
Our souls forever entwined.

And if we don't want hearts of ice,
We must pay the ultimate price
And love each other forevermore.
I don't mind because it is you I so adore.

a Journey of Love

All The Way

Hello again, I've missed you so very much.
I've missed your smile and your touch.
But, now that you're here, I can finally say
I love you and I want you to stay.

Lead me deep inside your core.
Show me how I can love you even more.
I feel the longing in my heart again.
I see your eyes saying yes, wanting to let me in.

In rhythm we could get lost in each other.
Never wanting to stop. No, not ever.
The softness of your lips, the feel of your thigh,
Make me feel lightheaded. A natural high.

The warmth of your special place
Heating me up, wanting to fill that space.
And when you say you're satisfied and smile,
I'll stay inside a longer while.

And as we lie side by side in embrace
I look at you and your beautiful face.
As the stars shine in the skies,
We look upon them with dreamy eyes.

I wish I may, I wish I might,
Be with you each and every night.
When the sun begins to rise
I want to see it's reflection in your eyes.

As you make your way through each day,
I want to be with you all the way.
I think of how lucky I must be
To have a divine spirit who loves me.

Tony Henninger

Never Say Goodbye

I have been dreaming of you again.
I was climbing over a rainbow to reach you.
For there you stood on the other side
Waiting for me to come to you.

You fell into my arms and I felt
As if I was holding heaven oh so tight.
We made love so sweetly, over and over.
Being in each others arms felt so right.

When I looked into your beautiful eyes
I got lost in them and where they led me.
I felt naked with my emotions on display.
Whenever I inhaled, I breathed you into me.

Then I was standing beside you
Kissing all of your tears away.
"You can believe in love again", I said,
As I took into my arms to stay.

Then, on a mountaintop we sat
And watched the world below.
One love, one heart, one life, one dream,
Was all we needed to know.

And with all this love in me and you,
And all we may ever do,

We will never say goodbye.

a Journey of Love

You Make It All O.K.

When I look at all the beauty around me,
I'm always looking at you.
When I think of where my life is heading,
I'm always thinking of you.
When I go to sleep and begin to dream,
I'm always dreaming of you.
When you are far away,
I'm always missing you.
When I feel I don't belong here,
I always belong with you.
When I feel cold and all alone,
I always want to be inside you.
When I need to be near someone,
I always need to be near you.
When I need to be loved by someone,
I always need to be loved by you.
When I need to head back home,
I always want to come home to you.
When I feel like life is killing me,
I always find strength in you.

I need all you can give to me
To make it through the day.
Knowing your love is there for me
Makes it all o.k.

Thank you for all that you are giving.
Thank you for what is yet to be.

But, most of all, I thank you
For giving your love to me.

Tony Henninger

I Love You

I will always want to
Tell you that "I love you".
That the nights are too long and
I'm cold here without you.
That is the worst feeling.

I know I will see you again,
But, my heart is still weeping.

I miss you when you're not here.
I ache for you when you're gone.
I feel so lost and helpless falling
Through this darkness alone.

Then I see the light of your love
Come rushing in to rescue my soul.
Taking me in your arms
And making me whole.

In letting me love you,
I'm always going to love you.

Now that I have found you,
I build my world around you.
I can feel our hearts beat as one
When yours is next to mine.

I can feel your body tremble
As it melts into my embrace.

a Journey of Love

I can see the want, the need,
In your dreamy looking eyes.
I can feel the slightest quiver
In the movement of your thighs.

And I want to touch you here.
And I want to touch you there.

Your eyes ever-changing
Like the colors of the rainbow.
I can see the love
And the passion they show.

When I look at you I see
The reason I love life so.

I want the world to know
I live to only love you.

I will always want to tell you
" I Love You."

With You

Safe Within Our Love

How did this miracle happen,
That we are so very blessed?
So close and content more than
I could have ever guessed.

I never thought that I
Could spend each precious minute
With just one person so special
And find happiness within it.

I have learned so much from you
About loving, sharing, and giving.
I know, if I had not met you,
I would not be really living.

We are facing life together.
We are handling joy and sorrow.
I am glad you're by my side
Whatever comes tomorrow.

You are my perfect partner.
My sweet lover and trusted friend.
We are safe within our love.
A love that will never end.

Tony Henninger

More Than My Dreams

In a land of forests and streams
We were holding each others hands
As through the lush grasses
Towards a waterfall we ran.

And I stood and watched
As you glistened in the sunlight.
Knowing I had never seen anything
More beautiful And I thought I might

Touch you and lick the water off
Your body and make love to you.
Your eyes reflecting a rainbow,
Its colors piercing me through.

The animals watching us at play
As we frolic among the rocks,
Swaying in tune to our motion
Like pendulum clocks.

And as we lie sated, side by side,
A cool breeze floats over us and away.
We revel in how sweet our love is
And wish we could forever stay.

Though the world was calling me
Back to its waking normality,
I woke from my blissful dream
And swore to make it a reality.

I know we don't have a waterfall,
No forests or glistening streams.
Yet, I still see, you are everything
And I love you more than my dreams.

Sea Of Dreams

You look so peaceful lying there
Asleep and dreaming.
As a smile crosses your face,
I wonder, are you dreaming
Of me?
When I am thinking of you
I seem to fly so far away,
Where nothing else matters,
Only the love in my heart
For you.
Every day is like a miracle.
You, lying there beside me.
As your eyes slowly open
They light the sky of my soul
Deep inside me.
Hold my hand as we stand
On the edge of the ocean of time.
Know that I am yours and
The ocean represents my love
Unending.

Tony Henninger

Fall upon me, take love from me,
Nothing is more beautiful to see.
Walk bedside me, drift into me,
All I am and all I will ever be you are
To me.
Believe in me and I will make you see
All the things your heart needs to know.
Because, where my love lies,
Only your eyes can ever see
So deep.
Swimming in a sea of dreams
You are floating in my arms.
You look so beautiful today,
I just have to say:
"I love you!"

A Moment In Heaven

How shall I describe my love for you?
It is softer than the plushest pillows.
It is warmer than any blanket.
It floats like the wind through the willows.
I LOVE YOU

It shines brighter than any sun.
It is deeper than any sea.
It makes me feel higher than any drug.
It is sweeter than any dessert could ever be.
I LOVE YOU

It is more beautiful than any flower.
It is larger than the skies above.
It is all I will ever, ever need.
So much more I could say, words aren't enough.
I LOVE YOU

Words sometimes fail me,
They can be so fragile and weak.
But, I'll keep on writing until
I find the words I seek.
I LOVE YOU

Tony Henninger

Every moment that passes by
When I'm lying next to you,
Is like a moment in heaven.
Lying on a cloud embracing you.
I LOVE YOU

Your eyes seem to look right through me,
Leaving nothing for me to hide.
Please, let me love you always.
And, always, be by my side.
I LOVE YOU

And as I write these words,
While watching you sleep,
I think of how blessed I am.
You hold my heart so very deep.
I LOVE YOU!

a Journey of Love

Nothing

Nothing is deeper

Than my love

For you.

Nothing is brighter

Than the flame I carry

For you.

Nothing can speak louder

Than my heart when I am

With you.

Nothing can love you more

Than my soul which I

Give to you.

Tony Henninger

You

You eyes
Make me want
To love you.
Your smile
Makes me want
To kiss you.
Your body
Makes me want
To touch you.
Your words
Make me want
To hear you.
Your tears
Make me want
To hold you.
Your heart
Makes me feel
At home.

YOU II

I look into the dark night sky
As the moon sheds his tears.
And all the stars that comfort him,
All the clouds that hide his fears.
I look upon the setting sun
As her colors clash with pride.
And her light warms my heart
With a love that will not subside.
I look into the ocean blue
As its enchantments swirl below.
What mysteries lie so very deep?
And shall I ever know?
As I sit beside you,
I begin to realize,
I see all of these wondrous things
Each time I look into your eyes.

Tony Henninger

Every Time

If every time you crossed my mind
A drop of rain should fall,
We could swim forever in
The greatest ocean of them all.

If every time I dreamt your face
A flower bloomed anew,
I could walk eternally
In my garden next to you.

If every time I saw you smile
A star was placed in sight,
Darkness would never fall upon
Our love's endless light.

If every time I needed you
A bird sang its song,
Our symphony would keep playing
Long after we are gone.

And because every time and all times,
I want you to be here
By my side for eternity.
I love you so much, my dear.

a Journey of Love

Realizations

Watching you,
I realize,
I am so in love with you.
Seeing you,
I realize,
No one else would ever do.
Listening to you,
I realize,
I love the words you say.
When I am with you,
I realize,
I always want to stay.
Fantasizing about you,
I realize,
I so want to make love to you.
Dreaming of you,
I realize,
My life is nothing without you.
Touching you,
I realize,
My senses become so heightened.
Being in your arms,
I realize,
I feel safe and not frightened.
When I am around you,
I realize,
I'm happy and never blue.
And after all this realizing,
I know,
My heart belongs to you.

I know, in my soul,
I will always love you.

Tony Henninger

Our Love - The Brightest Star

While you are sleeping
My eyes are drawn to you.
I see your beauty shine
As my dreams fall into you.
Lost inside your heart,
Like a child in paradise,
Wandering through your love
Under clear-blue skies.
Breathing in your scent
And touching all I see,
The rhythm of your body
Brings me to ecstasy.
Asleep in your heart
My dreams become reality.
Whether awake or asleep,
You are always my fantasy.
You know me so very well
And understand who I am too.
You are such a special woman.
You are my dream come true.
And then there is your smile.
So radiant, as you wink at me.
I think of how much I want you
While you reach for your tea.
Lying in my arms again
And returning to sleep,
I hold you tightly until
I hear you breathing deep.
My eyes are drawn to you again
As sleep begins to take me over too.
I seek out your lovely ear
And whisper, I love you.
Our love will shine like
The brightest star at night.

Reflection

When I look back on my life
I see a piece missing there.
I always felt lost and not quite right.
All my searching went nowhere.
Every time I look at you
Something inside me comes alive.
After all these years of searching,
I know, my soul mate has arrived.
When I look into your eyes
I see the man I want to be.
I see my happiness reflected there
In the love you have for me.
I thank God I finally found you.
I feel our hearts and souls are one.
My love for you will never end.
It glows brighter than the sun.
I feel so blessed to have you dear.
I love you more and more each day.
And in giving my heart to you,
You know, I'm yours in every way.
Every minute I'm away from you
Is a pain so hard to hide
Until I am with you again.
Holding you by my side.
I know there are things we must do,
Life isn't always fair.
It is just that missing you
Is the hardest for me to bear.
With your heart next to mine,
All my dreams of you,
All the love your giving me
Will always see me through.

Tony Henninger

Soul Mates

People are sleeping life away,
Like robots, their wires fray.
And love lies bleeding on the ground.
I am conscious of all I see,
Running in circles around me.
With you as my center, I am safe.
When my smile turns into a frown,
Catch me when I'm falling down;
Because, only you, can hold me up.
You pulled me out of my decay.
Showed me there was another way.
Like an angel come to rescue me.
And now we are together.
Our love will last forever.
A place of our own in paradise.
We are free, our hearts are bound
To each other. Such a lovely sound
As our hearts beat as one.
We do all we can.
Obey all the rules.
Our love won't ever waste away.
For we are Soul mates
You and I.

~ fini ~

Inner Child Press

Inner Child Press is a Publishing Company Founded and Operated by Writers. Our personal publishing experiences provides us an intimate understanding of the sometimes daunting challenges Writers, New and Seasoned may face in the Business of Publishing and Marketing their Creative "Written Work".

For more Information

Inner Child Press

www.innerchildpress.com

intouch@innerchildpress.com

Made in the USA
Charleston, SC
18 January 2013